JUNIOR MARTIAL ARTS
All Around Good Habits

Junior Martial Arts

ALL AROUND GOOD HABITS
CONFIDENCE
CONCENTRATION
HAND-EYE COORDINATION
HANDLING PEER PRESSURE
SAFETY
SELF-DEFENSE
SELF-DISCIPLINE
SELF-ESTEEM

JUNIOR MARTIAL ARTS
All Around Good Habits

KIM ETINGOFF

MASON CREST

Mason Crest
450 Parkway Drive, Suite D
Broomall, PA 19008
www.masoncrest.com

Printed and bound in the United States of America.

First printing
9 8 7 6 5 4 3 2 1

Series ISBN: 978-1-4222-2731-2
ISBN: 978-1-4222-2732-9
ebook ISBN: 978-1-4222-9065-1

The Library of Congress has cataloged the
        hardcopy format(s) as follows:

Library of Congress Cataloging-in-Publication Data

Etingoff, Kim.
  All around good habits / Kim Etingoff.
      pages cm. – (Junior martial arts)
    ISBN 978-1-4222-2732-9 (hardcover) – ISBN 978-1-4222-2731-2 (series) –
ISBN 978-1-4222-9065-1 (ebook)
  1. Martial arts–Juvenile literature. 2. Conduct of life–Juvenile literature I. Title.
  GV1101.35.E78 2014
  796.8–dc23
                                         2013004745

Publisher's notes:
The websites mentioned in this book were active at the time of publication. The publisher is not responsible for websites that have changed their addresses or discontinued operation since the date of publication. The publisher will review and update the website addresses each time the book is reprinted.

Contents

1

MORE THAN FIGHTING

Brushing your teeth. Doing your homework. Being nice to your little brother. What do all of these things have in common? They're all things you have to do a lot. They're all good habits.

There are many ways to learn good habits. Martial arts are just one way. Martial arts can teach you lots of good habits. Your martial arts teacher might not talk about doing school homework in class—but martial arts can teach you **skills** that will help you do your homework.

For example, you'll learn how to **concentrate**. That means you'll learn how to pay attention in martial arts class. You'll also be better at concentrating on your homework or in school.

Each kind of martial art is different. Aikido is all about using another person's strength against him. Students learn to grab and throw people who are trying to punch or kick them.

8

That's just one example. There are lots and lots of things martial arts teach you besides punches and kicks.

Self-Defense

All martial arts are used for **self-defense.** You learn how to defend yourself if someone is attacking you.

There are all kinds of martial arts. Some focus on throwing people who are attacking you to the ground, like judo. Others use a lot of kicking, like taekwondo. And others use weapons, like kung fu.

Martial arts aren't used for fighting though. You never use them to attack other people. You don't fight with your friends. You only use martial arts if someone is going to hurt you.

Even then, you should never try to hurt someone with what you learn in martial arts class. The point of martial arts is to be able to get away from an attacker. You want to fight back, but only so that you can get away.

You'll learn all about self-defense in martial arts. You might learn how to defend yourself just using words. If a bully is being mean to you, for example, you don't use martial arts. You learn how to use words to stop him and to get away. You don't try to hurt him.

You'll practice martial arts a lot in class. And you'll get really good. But you probably won't use them outside of class. But if you ever are attacked, you'll know how to defend yourself!

Martial Arts Around the World

There are martial arts from all over the world. Many of them are from Japan. Karate, jiu-jitsu, and aikido are from Japan. Taekwondo is from Korea. Kung fu is from China. Muay thai is from Thailand. There are martial arts from Europe, like fencing and boxing. And there are martial arts from South America, like Brazilian jiu-jitsu and capoeira. You can find classes in all those martial arts and more in lots of places around the world.

It can take a while to build good habits. You've got to keep trying, though. Remind yourself again and again that you want to stick with your new good habit until you don't have to think about it.

New Skills

Self-defense isn't the only thing you learn in martial arts, though. You learn all sorts of other things too.

You learn how to be a better person. The skills you learn in martial arts will help you be a better martial artist. But you can also be a better student, a better friend, and a better family member.

When you take martial arts, you learn how to be **confident**. That means you learn how to feel good about what you can do. You'll want to try new things and can even stand up to bullies.

You'll learn how to be responsible. Being responsible means you can make good choices. People trust you to make the right choices. Taking care of a pet is responsibility. Doing your schoolwork takes responsibility. So does doing chores for your parents.

Martial arts can teach you how to be **self-disciplined**. You're self-disciplined when you can make yourself do things that are good for you. You might not really want to do something—but you know it's good for you, so you do it. Doing homework is a good example. Practicing an instrument or following the rules in gym class also takes self-discipline. Self-discipline means sticking with something even when it's hard.

Martial arts teach you respect. Respect is thinking about people's feelings and being nice to others. Listening to your teacher shows you respect her. Being nice to your friends shows that you respect them. Doing what your parents ask you to do shows you respect them.

These are just some of the things you learn from martial arts. Once you start practicing martial arts, you'll see how they affect the rest of your life.

Good Habits

All these new skills lead to good habits. Habits are things we normally do a lot. We do them without really thinking about it.

There are good habits and bad habits. Everyone has some bad habits. Eating candy every day is a bad habit. It can make you sick and it's not good for your teeth. Another bad habit is picking on your younger sister. You might not think about how it makes your sister feel. But you might still do it anyway.

Good habits help you be happier and healthier. Brushing your teeth every day is a good habit. Your teeth stay healthier if you stick with brushing every day. Doing your homework is another good habit. You'll learn more and get better grades.

Martial arts can help you get rid of bad habits and start good ones. It's not always easy. But you can do it!

GOOD HABITS & MARTIAL ARTS

Y ou can learn lots of good habits in martial arts. It doesn't matter what kind of martial art you practice. Karate, judo, Brazilian jiu-jitsu—all of them teach you important skills.

Being on Time

The most important thing in any martial arts class might be just to show up! You can't learn anything else if you're not there.

You probably go to martial arts class once or twice a week. It's usually on the same days every week.

At first, it might be hard to remember when you have class. Or maybe you just don't want to stop watching TV when it's time for class.

Imagine that you're always to late martial arts class. You miss the first twenty minutes of every class. Those twenty minutes are important! You learn every-one's names in those twenty minutes. And you start learning new moves.

You never know what's going on in class when you get there. So you're behind everybody else. You don't know the moves as well. And you don't know who any-one is.

After a while, you get used to going to class. You know when classes are. It's easier to stop watching TV and get ready.

Now you're on time for every class. You're even early to a few classes. You're ready to go when the teacher starts talking. Now you know what's going on in every class.

Being on time to school or martial arts class is important. Being on time shows other people that you respect them. You care about what your teacher says, so you show up for class on time. You care about your friends, so you come to their house to play when you told them you would.

Being on time will also help you. When you show up on time, you can learn more or have more fun. You won't miss anything if you show up on time!

Practicing

A lot of what you do in martial arts class is practice. You learn a new move. Then you practice it over and over again.

You get a lot of time in class to practice. Your teacher will come over and give you some tips on how to do your move better. Then you practice some more.

You might even practice at home. Class time just isn't enough! Maybe your teacher gives you homework to practice. Or you just want to practice to get better.

Without practicing, you can't get better. Practicing is just trying a move again and again until you know how to do it. Practice helps your body and brain get used to doing the move. After a few hours of practicing, you can do something new.

It might take a couple days to do something new right. Or a couple weeks. It might even take a couple months. But just keep practicing!

Learning any kind of martial art can be hard work. Martial arts can teach you a lot about sticking with something even when it's not easy. Learning to push yourself and keep going is just one of the great things martial arts can teach you.

Good Habits & Martial Arts

Stress-Free

Do you ever feel stressed out? You feel **stress** when you're really worried about something. You feel bad when you're stressed. You might have a headache. Or feel sick to your stomach. You might have a hard time thinking of anything besides what's stressing you out.

You can be stressed from a test that's coming up. A fight with a friend or your family can stress you out. A big soccer game you're playing in can make you feel stressed too.

There are lots of things that can stress you out. But martial arts teach you how to deal with stress.

People feel better when they do **physical** activity. And martial arts are a lot of physical activity! Moving around makes our brains and muscles happier. We feel less stressed out after doing something like martial arts.

You might also learn how to meditate in class. Meditation is when you only think about one thing for a long time. Maybe you think about breathing.

Meditation is a way to relax and let go of stress. When you only think about your breathing, you can't think about anything else. You won't think about your stressful test or fight or game.

Once you stop meditating, you'll be calmed down. You won't be as stressed out as you were before you started meditating.

A lot of martial arts classes have students meditate for a few minutes. Your teacher might have everyone meditate for the last five or ten minutes in class. It will calm everyone down. And you'll be ready to face whatever is stressing you out!

Listening to Others

You're not going to get very far in martial arts if you don't listen to the teacher. She has a lot to teach you. But you can only learn if you're listening.

Listening to the teacher means not talking while she's talking. You don't talk to your friend who's standing next to you while the teacher's speaking to the class.

You sit or stand facing the teacher. You think about what she's saying. You could be thinking about a hundred other things, but instead you focus on your teacher. You want to learn what she's teaching! So you pay attention.

When you're practicing, you listen to other people too. Your teacher will come over and help you do some things better. You shouldn't get mad that you're not doing the move perfectly. You should listen and learn.

Older kids in class might help you too. Listen to them! They've already learned what you're trying to learn. So they have helpful things to say. If you listen to them, you'll learn even faster.

Listening in Sparring

In martial arts class, fighting with another student for practice is called sparring. Sparring has rules. The point isn't to hurt the other person. Sparring is a way to practice doing moves fast. You make choices about what moves you need to use.

In karate, sparring is called kumite. You use karate moves to fight with another person. You have to listen to other people when you are practicing kumite. You have to listen to make sure you're not hurting the person you're sparring with. If the other person says she's hurt or shouts, pay attention!

Making Goals

Every martial arts student makes goals. Goals are things you want to do. In martial arts, your goal might be to learn a new move. Or show up to class on time every day. An even bigger goal would be to get to the next level in your martial art. Or to be a martial arts teacher someday.

When you make goals, don't make them too hard. Don't tell yourself you want to get your black belt in six months. It can't happen. You have to work hard for a few years to get your black belt. If your goals are too hard and you don't reach them, you'll feel bad.

Make goals you can reach. Maybe you think you can move up one level in six months. You'll have to work hard. But you can do it!

You go to every class. You listen to the teacher. You practice at home. And soon, you're getting better and better. After only five months, you make it to the next level. You did even better than your goal!

IMPROVING YOUR GOOD HABITS

Martial arts can help you make good habits. But there are other ways too. You can practice good habits all the time, whether you're in a martial arts class or not.

Write It Down

A good way to keep up with good habits is to write things down. It's harder to forget to do things if you write them down.

Do you have a hard time remembering when you need to go to martial arts class? Or when your tests at school are? Write them down! Keep a calendar with everything written on it. Keep it somewhere you'll see it so it's easy to remember to look at the calendar.

It might be more fun to play with a friend than to do your homework. But if you finish your work first, you can play as much as you want without worrying about school.

Do you want to remember to brush your teeth twice a day? Write it down on some sticky notes. Put the notes on the bathroom mirror. Every time you see a note, you'll remember you need to brush your teeth.

The more you do something, the faster it becomes a habit. Habits are things we do without really thinking about them. So at first, you have to think hard about remembering to brush your teeth. Then it will just become a normal part of your day. It will be a habit.

Don't Put Stuff Off

Putting off important things you need to do isn't a good habit. It might be fun to play outside instead of doing your homework, but that's not a good idea. You won't make good habits if you put off doing things.

Martial arts classes won't let you put off hard work. In class, you have to do what the teacher says. You move around a lot. You think about new moves.

But at home, it's easier to be lazy. You might watch hours and hours of TV. Maybe you want to play on the computer instead of doing chores. Maybe you want to hang out with friends.

Putting things off or getting **distracted** gets in the way of doing what you need to do. Are you playing a computer game instead of doing your homework? Are you playing with friends instead of doing chores at home?

Practice doing the things you have to do first, before you do the fun things. You might not want to. But if you do your homework now, you don't have to do it later. And your homework has to get done.

Do homework as soon as you get home from school. Wait to play video games until your homework is done. Do chores first thing in the morning on weekends. Then you can hang out with friends.

You won't be worrying about doing all the things you have to do if you finished them earlier. They'll be done. No one will yell at you to do your homework or chores if you've finished them!

Fixing Bad Habits

We all have a few bad habits. We might watch too much TV instead of exercising. We may eat unhealthy food. Maybe we forget to say "thank you" sometimes.

Bad habits can be hard to fix. But you can work hard to turn bad habits into good habits!

Think about your bad habits. Is there one you want to fix? Write it down on some paper. Hang the paper up where you can see it. Whenever you look at the paper, you'll remember that you're trying to fix the bad habit.

Every time you think you're going to do your bad habit, stop yourself. It will take a while before you don't have to think about not doing it. It will probably be three to four weeks before you break your bad habit.

Martial arts can teach you a lot about respecting others and listening. In martial arts class, you have to listen to your teacher. That's a skill that can come in handy in school or with your parents, too.

Let's say you want to stop drinking soda. Your dentist just told you that you have a cavity. It might be because you drink two sodas every day. You don't want to get another cavity. So you want to stop drinking soda.

You write down your goal and hang it on the fridge. Every time you open the fridge, you'll see the paper.

At first, it's hard not to drink soda. You go to the fridge at lunch because you want to drink a soda. Then you remember you're not drinking sodas anymore. You have some juice instead.

You want some soda after dinner too. But you tell yourself you can't have any. To stop thinking about it, you do something else, like read or play video games.

The first week is hard. You end up drinking a soda once. You feel bad, but it's okay to make a mistake once in a while.

The second week is easier. You don't want soda so much. You're getting used to drinking juice, water, and milk.

You don't even think about soda after that. You forget that you ever drank so much soda. You got rid of your bad habit! And you turned it into a good habit—drinking more water.

Taekwondo Good Habits

Taekwondo is full of good habits. Not moving our bodies around much is a bad habit many people have. Many kids don't get enough exercise. The kicks and other moves you learn in taekwondo help you get the exercise you need. Lots of taekwondo teachers also teach students about eating healthy and drinking enough water. If you eat healthy, you'll be better at taekwondo. In taekwondo, students learn to focus on what they're doing. Before you even start learning moves, you learn to meditate. You'll learn how to relax and clear your thoughts. In taekwondo, an empty mind (when you're not thinking about anything) is called moo shim. Then you practice your moves slowly and thoughtfully. You pay attention to details about how your body is moving. Taekwondo, like many other martial arts, can be a great way to learn good habits!

Improving Your Good Habits   **23**

4

GOOD HABITS
&
YOUR LIFE

Good habits are great things to have. They're called *good* habits for a reason! Having good habits makes you healthier. It helps you do better in school. And it helps you have better relationships with your friends and family.

Health

Lots of good habits are about being healthier. And when you're healthier, you're happier. You aren't sick all the time. You don't have to go to the doctor or lie around in bed. If you have good habits now, you'll be healthier and happier when you get older too.

Are you learning about drinking lots of water in martial arts class? That's a good habit to have because it keeps your body healthy enough to do martial arts. It also makes you healthier all the time.

Drinking lots of water keeps your brain and muscles working. That way, you can play sports, take walks, and think clearly all the time.

Learning how to stay away from stress is healthy too. In martial arts class, staying calm helps you do moves better. You're thinking about how to do the move perfectly, not all the things that stress you out.

Outside of martial arts class, staying away from stress is a good idea too. Stress can make you feel sick. It can give you headaches or stomachaches. It can make you sad all the time.

So if you learn how to not get stressed out, you'll be better off. You won't get sick from stress. And you'll be a lot happier.

Martial arts are about moving your body and being in shape. Exercising is one of the best ways to stay healthy. Martial arts teach you about moving your body in new ways.

Learning martial arts teaches you about exercise. Making exercise a habit when you're young will help keep you healthy for the rest of your life!

Healthy Jiu-Jitsu

Jiu-jitsu is a great way to exercise and learn healthy habits. You don't have to be really strong to do jiu-jitsu. A small person can learn how to fight with a much bigger person. Each jiu-jitsu class starts with stretching. That's a good habit that warms up your muscles and keeps you from getting hurt. Then you practice new moves. You move around a lot, which is good for your heart. At the end of the class, you practice fighting. You learn not to hurt other people while fighting. That's a good habit you can use all the time!

Martial arts students learn a lot about how they can stay healthy while exercising. Students learn to stretch before working out and drink plenty of water. These healthy habits can help you for the rest of your life!

School

Many of the good habits you learn in martial arts really help you out in school.

If you've practiced good habits in martial arts, you can practice them in school too. Think about what you want to get better at in school. Do you want to get a better grade in social studies? Do you want to speak more in class? Do you want to finish all your homework?

Good habits help with all those things. To get a better grade in social studies, you have to listen to the teacher more. He'll tell you what you need to know.

You've already learned how to control your stress in martial arts class. Now you can use what you know to stay calm about talking more in class.

And maybe you can set goals for doing your homework every day. Write down your goal and put it where you normally do your homework. Remind yourself to do your homework every day. At first, it's hard. But then it becomes a habit!

Good habits make gym class and sports better too. When you have healthy habits like drinking water, you can move around better. You'll be a better athlete.

You'll pay attention to your gym teacher or coach. Then you'll know what's going on and can follow directions.

If you have sports practice, you have to be on time for it, just like with martial arts. Martial arts can help you get to practice on time.

Good habits help with music too. If you play an instrument, you know you have to practice a lot. You might not always want to practice when you should. In martial arts, you get used to practicing. It ends up being easier for you to practice other things, like instruments.

Friends and Family

Getting along with friends and family can be hard. It's not easy to think about other people's feelings sometimes.

Good habits help you get along with people, though. Remember how good you are at listening to your martial arts teacher? And your teacher at school? You can also listen to your friends and family.

Pay attention if your sister says you're being mean to her. Listen to your friend when he's having a bad day. Your sister and friend will thank you. They could have gotten mad at you for not listening. But you listened, and they're happier.

You'll also get along with people better if you're not stressed out. When we're stressed out, we sometimes snap at people. We get mad at them more because we're not happy. Or we stay away from people. We don't want to talk to others because we're stressed out.

When you know how to deal with stress, people will want to be around you more. And you'll want to be around more people. You won't get mad at them for no reason. And you'll want to talk to more people.

We all want good habits. Whether it's being on time for things or washing our hands, good habits are important.

You can learn good habits everywhere you go. Martial arts class is one place where you'll learn a lot of good habits. Then you can use them in school, at home, or wherever! You'll be happier and healthier with some good habits under your belt.

Words to Know:

concentrate: To focus on one thing.

confident: Showing others that you feel good about who you are and what you can do.

distracted: Having a hard time focusing or having your attention drawn to something other than what you're doing.

physical: Having to do with the body.

self-defense: Stopping another person from hurting you and making sure you're safe from danger.

self-disciplined: Being able to push yourself to do something even when you don't really want to do it.

skills: Things you learn that help you become a better person or live a better life.

stress: Feeling worried about things or like you have too much to do or think about.

29

Find Out More

ONLINE

Kids Ask Sensei
www.asksensei.com/kids.html

Kidshealth: Stess
kidshealth.org/kid/feeling/emotion/stress.html

KidzWorld: Martial Arts Quiz
www.kidzworld.com/quiz/5917-quiz-martial-arts-trivia

IN BOOKS

Huebner, Dawn. *What to Do When Bad Habits Take Hold*. Washington, D.C.: Magination Press, 2009.

NeonSeon. *Life of Shouty: Good Habits*. Atlanta, Ga.: Rixkin, 2009.

Safe Kids USA. *Self-Defense for Kids*. Austin, Tex.: High Mountain Publishing, 2009.

Scandiffio, Laura. *The Martial Arts Book*. Toronto, Ont.: Annick Press, 2010.

Index

31

About the Author

Kim Etingoff lives in Boston, Massachusetts, spending part of her time working on farms. Kim writes educational books for young people on topics including health, nutrition, and more.

Picture Credits